Unpublished Poems

by

Broc Rossell

Brooklyn Arts Press · New York

Unpublished Poems
© 2012 Broc Rossell

ISBN-13: 978-1-936767-04-5

Published in The United States of America by:
Brooklyn Arts Press
154 N 9th St #1
Brooklyn, NY 11249
WWW.BROOKLYNARTSPRESS.COM
INFO@BROOKLYNARTSPRESS.COM

Distributed to the trade by Small Press Distribution / SPD
www.spdbooks.org

Cover art by Aaron Sing Fox. Book design by Joe Pan Millar.

SECOND PRINITING

for Lara

CONTENTS

SANS MAISONNÉE

The end of this poem
Is beyond me
And in this discursion
You have joined yourselves
To an old certainty:

We love each other.
Fruits swell on branches
Out of the white blossoms of your
Freckled countries

While bats flow
Into the bright failure of themselves,
Wings beating echoes
Of this poem's lines
The tip of my tongue is tracing
On a winter windowpane.

In a new stanza
We are pared down
To the throat bone's thrumming;
We're in an octave people can't sing.

SMOKE

Where have I gone
That I didn't at the last turn
Against the idea of magnitude
Toward clouds instead

Implacable the horse bestirs
The bonnet
The bondsman
In his quiet moment
Behind the teller's window
Opening into
Jim Harrison's foxes

Onto the silent
Salt-lit days after the divorce
Onto the apricots
Onto elephants

Days that opened into windows,
Windows that opened
Upon the vistas
You posit behind each syllable

Each stone
In a creek bed
Circling the larger idea of land
Wizening grass-like aspirations

Into the ambition
Of utterance
Outlining the way
Scree runnels down to timber

Declaiming its silence
By standing
Each tree defying the sun
Knock it down
With my family
With my time alone

The moment I end is happening
It is the eternal
Voice that says "wait"
"Come any closer and you will leave your feet behind"

THE EROICA,
   or, EVEN HE WHO SOUGHT REFUGE IN NOBILITY MUST
   NEEDS RECOGNIZED IN A TORN SCORE THAT THE ENEMY
   MUST BE PURGED FROM HIS VERY SWORD

Spinning in a drum

Sun low in the old window glass

Furtwängler defeating Hitler in Vienna 1952

What is the poetic context

Spinning in a drum

                    *

It is darker
The spider rising on legs long as bridges' spans

I always seem to be able to keep a desk
Or a plank for a desk
Or forage in the alley for fruit

GRACE

you cannot escape   these
dreams,   even
if my   broken
beaming brain

puddles
itself
under my   body

my hands
are dry, your
hair still   growing

SUMMER FIRES

Beyond the flaming pines
I stood selling melons
Perpendicular to everything I love
Each melon like a note from the Diabelli Variations
Into this smoking dark world

The sky still blue
I flowered above the smoke
My skull turned into paper
Fingers elongated El Greco

Lurch-sailing through a thorny crowd
And home with a truck bed of melons

The driveway at dusk is the real home the home sits next to

On each brown brick a mute brown bird
Struck and still like hammers on strings
As in the white air to every black branch
Art lost, and lost, and lost

A CLOUD OF FAITHFUL WITNESSES

Hope is a form of penance

Like an oil rig
Spouting as it bores,

I climb to discover the rock

Or the Virgin of Guadalupe visits
And labor assumes a purpose.

Romance purports a dialectic between loss and solace

But this clerestorial poem
Has no house

Admits no refuge
Denies anything I can remember

MY BODY BECAME EAVES

The fraught wants more
Wants it strict and square
Like harmony's pinned note
All the wood is planed
All the cobwebs are empty cobwebs heavy with dust

Ferns cover this
But the trees have grown too tall
This has met the disfavor of the ferns
They swoled a promise, bad babies
They spin gray broadleaves out of that

I am strong not joyful
I run like a cup and a rabbit

Object, you can't make me lonely

    hylé

Somehow the water's listing plane is an uniformity
Its single dimension its own alternation
Facets and ridges echoing shadows on the water
Puckered draws of water between an eel's tail and its wake
Shallow shadow trimmed and animated
Shadows are formed and modified swiftly by bright surfaces

    hylé

The calyx –

Not the wind
Which contains it

Its blossom

In something silent:
Hounds of joy, an open wide eye

In a blossom's dead calm
Surrounding my slender body

A lancet of fire
That draws the pond dry

hylé

All like a saw
That bit like bells
Up into my flaring bright orbit

That unlocked desert, stripped and soft
Children endlessly born of chalk

hylé

You are only words
And you need the shore

I approve
No world for me

Not one best atom
No defense to think

I appeared between voices
I'm with less through this

You're: laughing
And a drink

> *hylé*

All you spent
Escapes if I write

A poem loses an idea
A weight
From me

> *hylé*

Today was not winter

Fog

A black-and-white sailboat

Casts off from a small marina

Whiskey percolates

The boat sails

I become the poem

hylé

Again my body became eaves

Voices intentions plumes

They curled my words back into my face

Fingers tripping
Through my beard

Cypresses wilting   windows and owls

Polyester pillowcases
Ambient sour light   rising from the street

From the half-carved block
In shards against the ocean my city
Where things become each other more slowly

hylé

The most valuable part of company is humor
The honest confusion of facts spoken in a joyful spirit

If this could be stasis
I would marry my neighbors
I would plant trees and walk through the forests

BEREFT OF COUNSEL

When we lack awe

The tragedy speaks

Truth

The age

Well-crafted

Re-write the tradition

Entertain

No idea

Hopes to be read

The sea

Queen of a hundred streams

LAC VIRGINIS,
　　　　or, *LA NUIT FAITE DE BRIQUES*

Sun in granular ruin

Bicycle fenders
Mottled blank

Tree branches bowed under a crown weight of silver

Electric lights bound
In sickly circumferences

While the minor tundra despairs
What it can't paint white:

A heliotrope
Fingering itself under a streetlamp

HELICOPTERS

My idea of morning has come full circle.
Today I am surrounded by another spring;
Rivers cast off the crystal-white robes of sleep –
We mark these beginnings with water
For the same reason romantics say the soul is in the eyes:
Translucence is the metaphor of the mind.

And what we might name the morning of the mind
Was born the moment man first drew a circle,
Precision ineffable as the cynosure of the uttered I
Referring only to its old self, as a sea speaks of its glacial spring
In the returning roar of the shore's white waters,
A longing so inexhaustible it sends us to sleep.

– The last mystery left to us, to say: *I slept.*
Others say not sleep but water is the bone yard of the mind,
For the mind is endlessly other, like water.
It's difficult to speak of such things without running in circles.
But a spiral, such as poetry, winds outward like the helical spring
Issued from each stone, each word, each luminous, liminal eye.

Mark the sign: in the center of the human eye
Darkness diminishes, but never sleeps.
In that void your thought lies in wait to spring
Out of the closet of your anguished mind
In orbit aloft like a seagull circling
Above tumescent water.

If the mind is a sea, then intelligence is water,
The intelligence that falls from our eyes
As it fell into them, the perfect circle
Invisible and vast in a universe asleep
But for its firings and collapses, dreams in a mind
From which stars eternally spring.

And still this morning our planet bequeaths another spring.
Ice unlocks itself, sets free its twin, and water
Flies to join clouds that are suddenly, seasonally of the same mind.
Before the bathroom mirror I look myself in the eye
After another night of fitful sleep,
And feel both bodies synced circadian in the cycle,

Unaware that in the cycle's circle everything is a false spring,
That we sleep more deeply with each glass of water,
Or that the irides of my eyes disclose the order of your mind.

PUTTING OUT THE CONSCIENCE LIKE AN INFINTESIMAL
	CIGARETTE

What is broken
		when one falls
				and the overseer
						maintains efficiency

The body
		doesn't even leave perspiration
				on the floor
						of the glacial plain

Who will aid the one
		who follows me
				will spell them at ten o'clock
						will make a motion make a noise

The world is an automobile
		the world is a peach pit
				the vanishing of human presence
						is a ripening fruit

The sun is not light
		but fire
				names faces words
						fathers and sons

Tribes and valleys
		customs and wine
				another convenient amnesia
						another ornamental blessing

Another payment of alimony
		and various tithes of breath
				one moment the wind
						is infected and the next

It smells like cocaine
		I say this without emotion
				from the promontory
						of my passable appointment

EACH SIN IS A DISAPPOINTMENT

There are ways of revising
The heart held is a thicker thing

Now the victim quivers between the shape of a child and that of a sandstorm

There are people like you
Who don't lay siege to castles then collapse like pennants lank and flat

Because your hands are trailing waves of watery light
Like the *Guinness Book of World Records* longest fingernails drill bit tendrils
Your fingers trace one white skim of the night tide along Mozambique or Cali

There is a simulacrum of that truth in most software applications

Also where there was a field
Fallen arrows swelled and grew

And there are the flumes from spent candles
Tunneling into the dreams of mice and into the soft dark toes of trees

And there are propensities bulging
Between bicycles and crop dusters

Dianas of your daydream
Globéd noumenons
The waterbugs in momentary trees

VESTIGIAL

When you fell into your feet
The torso tied off
And the night crept into another small country of grief

I walked from room to room
Flipping switches

Taking things from drawers
And bringing cups into the kitchen

Like a tree whittled down
To the handle of a bucket

Whittled by the wind over the gray green sea
That prunes each of these afternoons

Cleaned, then cooked
Down to something almost useful

Though you are no longer here to see
What remains of me
When I'm paying for this whole apartment

In a world where night begins
Among the grasses

And you rise from the ground
A reclamation of speech

SUNLIGHT ON SYMBOLIC LOGIC

To act -

Sail above the sailor
Fringed with lit fast cloud, happily toward

Island, some bright brigand
Given to cisalpine grandeur,
A house below the queen
Birthing her whip-white retinue

Tripping down the distance to the plain,
To the shore of the sea,
Full of a poem, a mind, of nothing but air

Ships fill the sea less than pebbles in a stream
Sailors filling ships like breadcrumbs in a toaster

One word for their benediction
One beat on a drum
To the blind eye in the blue sky
Its broken pupil, our black sun

Do I hold the ruined foot
Do I hold the tattooed hand
Do I trace with my finger the remains of your ablated arm

Your face
Is the body
You tread

Your face is the answer that belongs to no poem

My finger on your cheek my word in your mouth

To know -

O stranger
Careless blossom
Tall green stalk walking on your tiny knives

May I write with your body
May I speak in your presence and sound a note
May I turn from this wall and witness in silence your little blue flame

Stranger among strangers swimming toward land
A shining shim in the water of speech

In my hand I see yours
Unfurl its pearly lie
I praise with singing the air in your blood

Possible
Possible

It *is* possible

There eye sockets in the sky
Animals in my arms
Children in our hearts

Bright nightmare swelling the hearts of our children into variable stars

Consuming their bodies with a disease of energy

Some revenge of the sun upon the greediness of grasses

Some delight so sincere that our future is changed

To be alone -

The attitude of great poets is to single out each one of us
Silhouettes afore the crepuscule
Feverishly pumping in a city park every time someone shields a child from gunfire

The sail above is the same simple halo
A kind of lantern some turn to discover

To decide -

You have an animal
You watched and still wait
You fail to speak

My pride as yellow as a salamander's skin
Or the weeds that live in shadows

I hear low sounds, the high range fading into sky
I open myself selectively

I roll in a cloud of feathers through the thoroughfare
I plant myself with ears and brace for the onslaught of the thoroughfare

From a place where change is just a thing about time
To home

You witness my shadow
The Caravaggio in the corner of Hopper's barn

You have an animal in you is not something we can bear
You have an animal in you is something we wait to hear

To believe -

Inviolable Mother, you do not speak for your children
Who scrabble in the dirt with buildings brushes and pens
Raising scars like mountain ranges on swaths of flat silence
Like the girl parking her 2007 sedan between errands
Or the boy recalling the man who only robbed him of half his ration of rice
Our silence is failure
Failure is reverence to you

THE RAIN SEEDS A BODY AND AN INVISIBLE BODY

I am a quiet

And false alibi

The words you say

As apples drop

You are the darkness night recruits

In frightened pupils

And we are wedded to wet things

Flashing

Like spring or children

In late August

Who give heat its buoyancy

Screaming

TRUE SUPERSTITION IS IGNORANT HONESTY
& THIS IS BELOVED OF GOD AND MAN

The most one can manage
is the end of the moment –

the plough of bone
through incoming air.

Place yourself upon a bower
and wait for the signal

I can't say how many are coming
I don't know with what tools

they will wrap you in a sheet
and wrap the sheet around the branch of a tree

like a cyst in the sun.

I used to lay my skinny body down

on the sun-warmed concrete deck of the pool like a lizard,
rolling over to pock the other side of my body –

imagine the sun
denting you.

I feel my internals re-order like cornered animals

The songs I remember are for cowards

It is an astonishment to see large stones become smaller

One sustained fricative, as if through the trees

CONSCRIPTION

Resonant structures
I a stream between capital Ls and Ts
Three-story two-story six-story trees

A genuflective tributary
Where empire
Meets tribe

The shadow of Burj Khalifa
Lashing the gravestones
Of people my first boss killed

So many miles from the suburb
Of my language and my light

THE SIDE OF THE PAGE WITH INK ON IT

Giving what goes away,
A name of something, a face
On its core, its windspore, winding
From terra to terrace,

Earth takes of earth
What nurtures itself,
We speak of ourselves
On the tip of its tongue

Magma and temperature alone in the dark
Happily so
Enough with stars and instability
Enough of the digressions
That work on my heart,

Do not hearten me
Do not scold me with your kisses
Or caress me, stranger, with blows –
Lead me to the end
Where simplicity begins,
Begift the silence of a tired planet,

Let us wander
Far from the woken,
Far from the wonder of words.

NOTES AND ACKNOWLEDGEMENTS

I am grateful to the editors of the following journals, where poems from this collection have previously appeared, or will appear: *Colorado Review, Harvard Review, Memorious Magazine's blog, Octopus, Volt,* and *Volta* (*né Rabbit Light Movies*). Thanks, too, to John Wheeler-Rappe and Joe Pan at Brooklyn Arts Press, doctors who delivered this baby. And credit goes to Seth Landman, W. Scott Howard, and Virginia Jackson for suggesting some of the quotes on the back of this book.

"A Cloud of Faithful Witnesses" was the title of a sermon by the English Puritan William Perkins published the year John Robinson's congregation fled to Amsterdam.

In "Sunlight on Symbolic Logic," "Some revenge of the sun upon the greediness of grasses" borrows the phrase from Dan Beachy-Quick's poem "Arcadian" in *Circle's Apprentice.* "The attitude of great poets," according to Whitman, was "to cheer up slaves and horrify despots."

"True Superstition is Ignorant Honesty & This is Beloved of God & Man" is a bit of marginalia written by William Blake in a collection of aphorisms.

ABOUT THE AUTHOR

Broc Rossell was born in Los Angeles and lives in Vancouver, British Columbia. He attended the Iowa Writers' Workshop and is completing a doctorate in literature and creative writing. This is his first collection.

Made in the USA
Monee, IL
07 July 2026

56544781R00025